YUMA COUNTY LIBRARY DISTRICT

Teen Guide to
Saving and Investing

Stephen Currie

ReferencePoint Press®

San Diego, CA

© 2017 ReferencePoint Press, Inc.
Printed in the United States

For more information, contact:
ReferencePoint Press, Inc.
PO Box 27779
San Diego, CA 92198
www.ReferencePointPress.com

LIBRARY OF CONGRESS CATALOGING-IN-PUBLICATION DATA

Names: Currie, Stephen, author.
Title: Teen Guide to Saving and Investing / by Stephen Currie.
Description: San Diego, CA : ReferencePoint Press, Inc., 2017. | Series: Teen Guide to Finances | Includes bibliographical references and index.
Identifiers: 9781682820865 (hardback) | ISBN 9781682820872 (eBook)
Subjects: LCSH: Juvenile literature.

Contents

Early Start on Savings Pays Off

Experts often urge people to start saving money for retirement when they are still young. A retirement account such as a 401(k) or IRA earns interest, which adds up over time. The earlier a person starts investing in this type of account, the more interest accrues. This chart illustrates the difference that just ten years can make. It shows what happens when one person starts a retirement savings account at age twenty-five and the other starts the same type of account at age thirty-five. Although both began with the exact same amount of money, by age sixty-five Person #1 has almost twice as much wealth as Person #2. The difference is the extra ten years of accrued interest.

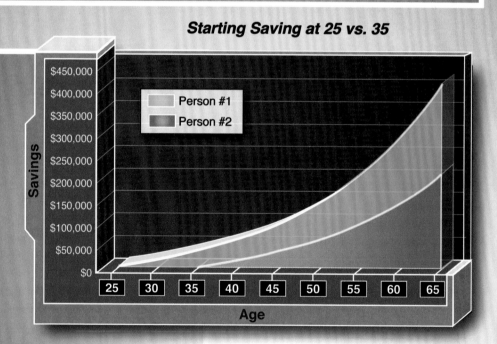

Starting Saving at 25 vs. 35

Legend: Person #1, Person #2

Savings axis: $0, $50,000, $100,000, $150,000, $200,000, $250,000, $300,000, $350,000, $400,000, $450,000

Age axis: 25, 30, 35, 40, 45, 50, 55, 60, 65

Source: Libby Kane, "These 3 Charts Show the Amazing Power of Compound Interest," Business Insider, July 8, 2014. www.businessinsider.com.

Chapter One

Why Save?

Books, magazines, and the Internet are full of financial advice for teens and adults: how to find jobs, how to create a budget, how to make sure to pay bills on time. One suggestion that comes up again and again is that people should save money—that is, anyone who earns money should put away some portion of those funds for future use. "Saving is the key to getting the things out of life that are important to you," says a financial literacy website called TheMint. Indeed, experts agree that saving money is essential for good financial health.

Saving Toward a Goal

Many people save money for a particular goal. A teenager with a part-time job might earn around $100 a week. That weekly paycheck is not enough to buy a piece of electronic equipment, a guitar, or a snowboard. If the teenager spends all of his or her earnings on fast food, gas and insurance for a car, and entertainment, there will be no money left over at the end of the week—and no opportunity to buy larger, more expensive items. To amass enough money to purchase a laptop, a bicycle, or a fancy pair of sneakers, let alone enough to buy a car, it is necessary to set aside some money each week.

Most financial experts encourage their clients to save money for special purposes such as these. It may be easier for teenagers, in particular, to save money if they have something specific in mind. "Specific saving goals give your teenager something concrete to work for," notes journalist Shelley Frost in an article aimed at parents and posted on the financial website Zacks. Though a pickup truck, even a used one, is far too expensive for the average high school student to purchase with the earnings from a single paycheck, buying a truck might be possible after a year or two of careful saving.

Saving for college is another common goal for high school students. College costs are high; one year at the University of Kentucky, for example, will cost a Kentucky resident close to $25,000, and private schools such as Duke University in North Carolina are even more expensive. Few, if any, teenagers can earn enough money to pay for all of their college expenses on their own. Some combination of parental help, assistance from scholarships, and student loans may be necessary to enable a teenager to attend—and graduate from—a two- or four-year college. Still, many high school students take pride in assisting their families by paying for some of their college expenses themselves, and saving is a way to make that possible. Just as teenagers often find it easier to save money if they have plans to buy something specific, such as a motorcycle or a new smartphone, the goal of saving

> "Saving is the key to getting the things out of life that are important to you."
>
> —Financial literacy website TheMint

6

for college can encourage high school students to put money away as they earn it.

Goals for Adults

Like teenagers, adults often save toward special goals of their own. However, meeting savings goals for adults, even young adults, is typically more complicated than it is for teenagers. Although adults make more money than teenagers, they also have much higher expenses. The great majority of Americans under age eighteen, for example, live with their parents. It is the parents' responsibility to feed, clothe, and house their children who are not yet adults. Although high school students might be expected to buy their own food when they are out with friends, for example, or to pay entertainment expenses out of their own pockets, it is not difficult for students living with their parents to be frugal. The same is not true of adults who are no longer being supported by their parents.

As a result, adults typically have much more significant savings needs than teenagers. Many high school students do not really need a car, for instance; but adults who live in places where public transportation is scanty often do require one to get to work. Cars are expensive, though. Even a high-mileage secondhand vehicle that needs some replacement parts may cost several thousand dollars. Like teenagers, adults often need to save toward this goal. (People who cannot pay the full price of a car can often get a loan, but loans generally require a down payment, which is a percentage of the total cost of the car. Down payments are due when the loan is issued.) Someone who is hoping to buy a car will have to determine how much he or she needs to save each month—and for how many months—in order to afford the down payment and be able to purchase the car.

Nor are cars necessarily the most expensive items or services adults need to buy. It is common for adults to save for even bigger purchases, such as weddings, college tuition for their children, or the purchase of a home. These purchases are not cheap. The typical American wedding, for example, costs at least $20,000, and it is not unusual for people to spend double that amount

The Marshmallow Experiment

Saving is hard work for many people, and a 1960s experiment carried out by psychologist Walter Mischel helps explain why. The study, known today as the marshmallow experiment, examined children's willingness to wait for rewards. Mischel offered preschool children a treat, such as a cookie, a pretzel, or a marshmallow. The children were told that they could eat the treat right away, but if they could wait fifteen minutes without eating the treat, they would be given an extra treat and permitted to eat both.

Mischel found that some children ate the marshmallow right away, but others tried very hard not to. However, only about a third of the children were able to last the entire fifteen minutes without eating the treat. The experiment is often taken as an example of how difficult it is to delay gratification. Just as children find it hard to ignore the marshmallow in front of them even though they know they will soon have twice as many marshmallows if they do so, children, teenagers, and adults can all find it difficult to save money toward a more distant goal when more immediate needs are competing for their attention.

when clothing, space rental, flowers, food, and other costs are taken into consideration. College can be costly too. And real estate is more expensive yet. As of early 2016, the median price of a home in Colorado—that is, the price that would be exactly in the middle if all homes on the market were listed in order of cost—was nearly $300,000. That amount is several times the annual income of the typical Colorado resident.

Given the reality of costs like these, the vast majority of American adults have no choice: if they wish to become homeowners, send their children to college, or pay for a big wedding, they must develop a plan to save toward that goal. Virtually no first-time homebuyer in Colorado—or, for that matter, in states where housing prices are considerably lower—can use a single paycheck to purchase a house or condominium. Nor can most American families write a check for a year's college expenses without having put money aside to do so. "Saving for college is critical," notes the New Parents Guide, a website offering advice and suggestions for parents of young children. Parents often assume that their children will qualify for scholarships, but that may not be the case: only 2 percent of students, the New Parents Guide article continues, actually get scholarship assistance. Without savings, college may be an impossibility.

Retirement

Finally, adults have another important financial goal that can only be met through saving. That is retirement. Most people stop working sometime between age fifty-five and seventy. They continue to receive income through a government program called Social Security, which gives retired workers a monthly payment based on the number of years they worked and the amount of money they earned when they were actively in the job market. (Some Social Security payments are given for different reasons, such as payments when younger people become disabled and can no longer work. In most cases, however, Social Security payments are made to those people who have worked for many years and are now retired.)

As of 2016 the average Social Security payment was about $1,300 a month. That is not enough for most people to live comfortably. It takes at least that much to ensure that retirees have enough for the basics of living—a home, a car, the ability to buy sufficient groceries and clothing—and more money still to be able to afford leisure activities such as travel, which workers often look forward to in retirement. "It's very difficult living on Social Security," says Barbara Woodruff of Missouri, who was interviewed for an article appearing on the website Grandparents.com. Woodruff, who retired in her early sixties, lives as frugally as possible, but she finds that some activities are beyond her means. "My social life is virtually non-existent," she says. "Going out for a drink or dinner, I just can't do that anymore."

> "It's very difficult living on Social Security. . . . Going out for a drink or dinner, I just can't do that anymore."
>
> —Retiree Barbara Woodruff

To avoid a situation like Woodruff's, most Americans try to supplement their expected Social Security payments with private retirement income. This involves setting aside money on a monthly or annual basis so it can be used later on. However, saving for a comfortable retirement is a much bigger goal than saving for a new cell phone or even a pickup truck. Workers may need to save several hundred thousand dollars over the years to fund their retirements. Unfortunately, many Americans are falling short of this goal. According to a 2016 survey described in *Time* magazine, more than half of American workers currently have less than $10,000 saved toward retirement—and about two-thirds of those say they have no retirement savings at all.

Emergencies

Saving—whether for big-ticket items like college, retirement, or a wedding or smaller items, such as shoes or sports equipment—is always a worthwhile goal. But smart savers also put money aside for no particular purpose. Instead, they save money in case they might need it in the future. This is frequently known as saving for a rainy day. Saving for this purpose is more valuable for adults than it is for most teenagers; for people under eighteen and those still living with their families, after all, most large expenses and many small ones as well are paid by parents. Still, even teenagers can benefit from saving money that is not earmarked for a specific goal.

Putting money aside for a rainy day means putting it aside for financial emergencies—situations in which people badly need more money, often in a hurry. By definition, emergencies do not happen very often. But when they do, they can be devastating to a person's financial health. "Who is going to pay that medical bill from when you broke your arm?" asks financial educator Mike Caira on the National Financial Educators website. "How about that new tire for your car when you accidentally ran over some nails left in the road near a construction

> **"Who is going to pay that medical bill from when you broke your arm?"**
>
> —*Financial educator Mike Caira*

A new guitar might be prohibitively expensive for a teenager who only has a part-time job. But having a specific goal in mind and then setting aside some money each week will help the teen save up enough money to eventually buy that guitar.

site?" A pet becomes quite sick and needs expensive veterinary care; changes at a workplace reduce a worker's hours or result in her losing her job altogether; a cell phone, no longer under warranty, is dropped into a pool and must be replaced. All of these events can hurt a person's wallet.

The money put aside in this manner may never be needed. But life is full of surprises, and the surprises are not always good ones. Most financial experts recommend that people determine how much money they can expect to spend in any given six-month period, and then put this much money aside in case income stops coming in due to job loss—or in the event that expenses suddenly increase. The reality, though, is that most Americans do not have this type of financial cushion. "Americans continue to show a stunning lack of progress in accumulating sufficient emergency savings," says financial analyst Greg McBride in *Time* magazine.

Some argue that young adults have particular trouble saving for a possible crisis, in part because younger workers have difficulty believing that emergencies can or will take place. "The younger a person is, the more immortal they feel," says credit union employee Andy Ramos in an article published on the Co-Op Credit Unions website. "This leads to younger Americans feeling like they can always start saving 'later.'" Too often this feeling of immortality means that people reach middle age and still have little saved up for an emergency. Feelings aside, many young people struggle financially as they begin their careers. High rents, low starting salaries, and

Savings and Aesop

Born in Turkey more than two thousand years ago, Aesop was a writer best known for his fables—very short stories with morals. Although money was much less common in Aesop's time than it is in our own, several of Aesop's fables deal with the importance of saving in other ways. One of his most famous fables, "The Grasshopper and the Ant," contrasts the actions of a grasshopper with those of an ant. The grasshopper, so the story goes, spends his summer dancing and singing happily while the ant industriously stores food for the coming winter. When winter arrives, the ant has plenty of food—and the grasshopper has none. The grasshopper begs the ant for food, but the ant refuses, telling the grasshopper that he should have planned ahead. The moral of the story is that preparing for the future is of vital importance; focusing only on the here and now and ignoring what might happen in the future is foolish.

the need to pay off student debt can all make saving difficult for many young adults.

Other experts, however, cite statistics suggesting that Americans who are younger than thirty actually do better at saving than older people. One study showed, for instance, that today's young adults started saving for retirement much earlier than was true in earlier generations. Whereas the average baby boomer (those born between 1946 and 1964) did not start saving for retirement until age thirty-five, 70 percent of employed young adults today have started saving for retirement by the age of twenty-two. This extra attention to savings might be because younger adults, sometimes called millennials, came of age during a recession, or economic downturn, that began in 2008 and has had significant effects ever since. "Millennials have seen what happened to their parents, many of whom lost their jobs and savings in the financial crisis," says researcher Catherine Collinson in an interview with *Time* magazine. "We're seeing an emerging generation of retirement super savers."

Regardless of which age groups are best at saving, experts agree that saving money is a good thing. Not only can saving permit people of any age to amass enough money to buy what they need and want, but saving can provide Americans with the cushion they need in the event of job loss, salary cutbacks, or unexpected expenses. Those who have money in savings are much better equipped to deal with these issues than those who have saved little or no money.

Chapter Two

How to Save

The idea behind saving money is simple enough: People who want to save only need to spend less money than they take in. Any money that is not spent automatically becomes a part of that person's savings. If a worker earns $1,000 a week, for instance, and spends an average of $900 each week, that leaves $100 that can be set aside as part of a savings plan. Over time, the amount of money saved will grow significantly. In the example above, a worker who saves $100 a week will be able to put aside more than $5,000 in the course of a year. (Fifty-two weeks, multiplied by $100, gives a result of $5,200.) And increasing the amount set aside each week will increase the amount saved in total.

For many Americans, though, saving is difficult. One issue is that many people, particularly adults, have expenses that more or less equal their entire income. In an interview with *Time* magazine, financial columnist Cameron Huddleston mentions "credit card debt, student loan debt, [and] low wages" as just a few of the reasons why saving can be difficult for many Americans. She notes that "all of these things can put a strain on our budgets."

When every penny seems earmarked for a necessary expense, it is difficult to put much money aside. But the trouble many people have saving money is not a simple matter of costs matching—or exceeding—income. Financial experts note that people often have difficulty planning ahead, saving can be slow to yield positive results, and many Americans do not receive much in the way of financial education in school or from their families. The result is that Americans often know that they *should* save—but do not know exactly how to do so.

Teenagers and Saving

Financial experts recommend that everyone—children and teenagers included—get into the habit of saving money. Though teenagers sometimes argue that saving is impossible for them given how little they can earn while going to high school or college full time, the reality is that anyone with any income can develop a savings plan. Nor does that income need to come from an official part-time job, such as working as a counselor in a day camp or waiting on tables at a restaurant. Money put aside for savings can also come from allowances given by parents or from odd jobs such as babysitting and lawn care. Plenty of teenagers get money as gifts, moreover, especially when graduating from high school or participating in coming-of-age celebrations such as a bat or bar mitzvah (given for Jewish children around the age of thirteen) or a *quinceañera* (held for some Latina girls when they turn fifteen).

Indeed, saving money can be especially important for teenagers precisely because their incomes are so low. Suppose that Thomas, a high school student, wants a new video game console. Consoles are expensive, so

A quinceañera provides an opportunity for a memorable portrait with family and friends. By setting aside gifts of money from events such as this or from holidays or birthdays, teens can make a good start at saving for future wants and needs.

Thomas is unlikely to be able to buy it with a single pay-check from a part-time, minimum-wage job. In this situation, he has two choices. If he spends all of his earnings on movie tickets, restaurant meals, and the like when he receives each paycheck, he will never get any closer to his goal of buying the console. The alternative is to spend less from each paycheck and put the rest of the money away. Thomas must make the deliberate choice to spend less on food and fun in the present in order to meet his goal for later on. In the long run, this is the best way for Thomas to get the console he wants.

Saving for a console—or any other item, for that matter—requires two basic pieces of information. The first is the item's cost, which can usually be found by looking online or in printed store advertisements. Thomas might see a console advertised at a nearby store for $229.99, for example. Adding in sales tax—an extra fee based on the cost of the item and charged on many purchases by most local and state governments—results in a total cost to Thomas of between $240 and $250. That cost may rise or fall by the time Thomas has enough money to purchase the console, of course, but $250 is a reasonable estimate. Thomas now knows that he must save approximately $250 in order to be able to buy the item.

Putting Money Aside

The second necessary piece of information where saving for a goal is concerned is how long it will take to save the money to buy the item in question. That will depend on a number of factors, including the amount of money that comes in each week and the length of time the consumer is willing to wait for the item. Suppose that Maliki, a college student with a part-time job, wants a leather jacket and finds one she likes at a local store for a total cost of $180. Maliki decides that she is willing to wait up to three months to purchase the jacket. Dividing $180 by 3 yields $60; thus, Maliki will need to put aside about $60 from her earnings every month in order to save $180 within her specified time frame.

529 College Savings Plans

College costs can be extremely high. As of 2016, several political candidates had advocated for legislation that would reduce or eliminate tuition costs for some students at certain public colleges and universities. But these ideas might never reach—or pass—Congress. In the meantime, students and their parents are forced to scramble to afford higher education, using a combination of savings, loans, and scholarships to make college possible.

In 1996 Congress set up a new type of savings plan designed to make saving for college easier. Known as a 529 plan, it allows people to set aside money when children are very young. The money can then be used to pay college expenses when the child is old enough to attend college. The amount of money people put into the plan can grow over time too, thanks to interest payments that add to the funds in the account. Ideally, the money saved in a 529 plan will be sufficient to enable a student to attend four years of school without any further outlay of cash—and without relying on scholarships or resorting to taking out loans. These plans have been helpful for many students and their families.

For many college students, saving $60 a month is a reasonable expectation. But in some cases, saving that much may not be realistic. Perhaps Maliki's monthly earnings come to less than $60, for instance. Or perhaps nearly all of Maliki's income goes for books, food, or rent, leaving little or nothing that can be saved toward the purchase of a jacket. In these situations, Maliki has several choices. She can try to increase her income by getting a second part-time job or increasing the number of hours she works at her existing one. She can settle for a less expensive jacket. Or she can continue to save toward the jacket she likes best, putting aside whatever she can each month and recognizing that it will probably take her more than three months to complete the purchase.

Maliki may have one final option as well. That is to cut her expenses. For instance, she might choose not to pay for cable service any longer, reasoning that she would rather have a leather jacket than access to reruns. She might add a roommate, meaning there would be more people to share in the rent, or buy used textbooks instead of new ones. Financial advisers generally agree that nearly everyone, including teenagers, can decrease their spending to allow them to increase their savings. "We can usually all find some way to spend less," advises the Commonwealth Bank of Australia on a webpage aimed at teenage savers. "If you go out with friends on the weekend, for example, you might need lunch. But do you really need to spend $10 on that lunch?" If packing a sandwich makes it possible to put aside a few more dollars toward the jacket she really wants, the sacrifice may well be worth it for Maliki.

> "We can usually all find some way to spend less."
>
> —The Commonwealth Bank of Australia

Fixed and Variable Expenses

Although American adults have greater earning power than teenagers, they also have higher expenses. Most adults, for example, must pay housing costs each month. If they rent an apartment or a room in someone's house, they owe rent to the owner of the building. If they own a condo or house, they generally get a loan from a bank or other financial institution to cover the purchase price and then pay the loan back each month over a period of many years. In either case, the payment amount is fixed and can often be large. In early 2016, for example, the average monthly rent for a one-bedroom apartment in San Francisco, California, was more than $3,000. It can be hard to save when housing costs are this high.

Nor are housing costs the only issue for American adults. Many took out loans to help them pay for their educations beyond high school. These loans must eventually be paid back, and a lot of adults pay hundreds of dollars a month toward their student debt. Other common expenses include monthly payments for cell phones and Internet connections and transportation expenses such as bus fare or car payments. Along with housing, costs like these are often known as fixed expenses because they do not vary much from month to month. A 2016 guide to savings on the website About Money, posted by financial expert Paula Pant, notes that "fixed expenses typically represent the biggest chunk of your budget."

> **"Fixed expenses typically represent the biggest chunk of your budget."**
>
> —*Financial expert Paula Pant*

Not all expenses are fixed. Other spending comes under the heading of variable expenses. Entertainment, such as tickets to movies or sports events, is one example of a variable expense. In some months an individual might spend hundreds of dollars on entertainment, but in other months entertainment costs might be near zero. Grocery and clothing bills likewise can rise and fall from one week, month, or year to the next. And although some variable expenses, such as entertainment, are at least partly under the control of the spender, others are not. Car repairs are a familiar example to any driver. It is entirely possible to go from January to May with no repair bills at all—only to be hit with an enormous invoice in June when brakes, tires, and hoses all go wrong at once.

Since fixed expenses are hard to reduce, financial advisers recommend that savers try to spend less money on variable expenses. "Whenever you're in a store and you pick up an item," suggests author Darryl Wortham in his book *Transforming from Consumer to Producer in 90 Days,* "hold it for ten seconds. During those ten seconds, ask yourself if you really need it." Most of the time, Wortham argues, the answer is no, and the money not

Around the World

College student Lauren Juliff had a dream of traveling around the world after she got her degree. Travel, unfortunately, is expensive, and Juliff's main source of money was $14,000 earned from a series of part-time jobs while she was getting her college degree. Given ordinary living expenses and the cost of travel, it seemed unlikely that Juliff could carry out her dream.

But Juliff was determined to make the trip, and she concentrated on saving as much money as she possibly could. Juliff set herself a goal of saving $500 a month. Though she did not always meet this goal, she came close. She bought no new clothes and watched movies at home rather than going to the theater. By not eating out and not buying drinks at coffee shops, Juliff estimated that she saved several thousand dollars a year. When tempted to make a purchase, Juliff would ask herself whether the item in question would make her as happy as her planned trip, and the answer was usually no. Juliff's perseverance and emphasis on saving paid off. Following graduation, she spent two full years traveling. Her savings had made the trip possible.

spent on the item can be put into savings instead. Even less-controllable expenses such as auto repairs can be minimized through such strategies as regular maintenance. Getting regular oil changes, for example, can significantly reduce the need for expensive engine repair.

Pay Yourself First

Saving money takes discipline. It is all too easy to spend money on nonessentials instead of putting it aside. Psychologists say that people are wired for instant gratification—they prefer to get something now rather than getting something better or more useful in the future. As an article on the *Entrepreneur* website defines it, "Instant gratification is the desire to experience pleasure or fulfillment without delay or deferment." Instant gratification does not easily coexist with the goal of saving money. People want immediate happiness, and saving requires them to take a longer view. No matter how much they may wish to become savers, people often succumb to the desire to get what they want right now—even if that means spending money that might be better set aside for another purpose.

To combat the desire for instant gratification, people often try to make it difficult to spend the money they wish to save. Financial advisers often suggest that people pay themselves first. That means setting aside money from every paycheck before any of the paycheck is spent. Suppose a worker receives a check for $3,400 every month and hopes to save $500 from each paycheck. That worker begins each month by putting $500 aside, most likely in a special bank account earmarked for savings, and then uses the rest to pay ordinary expenses, both fixed and variable—food, rent, clothing, transportation, and so on. By setting $500 aside first, the worker will be less tempted to use that money on other expenses.

The pay-yourself-first strategy is not always easy. Unexpected expenses can make it difficult to save as much money as a person might want. And it can be hard to change old habits. "There's an unwillingness to do something different if we've been doing it the same way for some time," points out financial planner David Blaylock in an interview with *Forbes* magazine. But the alternative to paying yourself first is paying yourself last—that is, spending most or all of a paycheck before saving anything. That method generally ends poorly, with little or nothing set aside and a feeling on the part of the would-be saver that he or she is making no progress. Trying to save, then, may be difficult. But the alternative—not saving at all—is considerably worse.

> **"There's an unwillingness to do something different if we've been doing it the same way for some time."**
>
> *—Financial planner David Blaylock*

Chapter Three

Banks, Credit Unions, and CDs

In earlier times, people who wanted to save money often did so, at least in part, by storing cash somewhere around their home: in a jar in the kitchen or in a box concealed below a garden wall. Although some people still do this, most do not. They might still have a change jar, however. Author Danny Iny, for example, used to immediately spend the coins he received from paying cash for various items. In 2015 Iny began putting all his coins into a special jar. In just seven months he had amassed over $700—money that became part of his savings.

It can be fun to toss coins into jars and watch the level of the coins rise over time. However, most Americans today prefer to use banks and other similar businesses to help them save. Not only is the use of a bank safer, but banks and other financial institutions can also offer incentives to those trying to save their money. In particular, they are able to add to the amount of money a saver has. Though these additions are usually small, every bit of extra money can help make saving a little bit easier.

Lending and Borrowing

The term *financial institution* can refer to a broad array of businesses, but to most people it refers to banks, credit unions, and other places that offer loans and take deposits of money. Banks have been in existence for hundreds of years. They were instrumental in the growth of Europe as a powerful continent during the Renaissance and afterward, and they have been vital in making the United States one of the world's richest nations. Banks are for-profit institutions; their goal is to make money for their owners. At the same time, bank officials seek to help others reach their own financial goals—while making sure that the bank continues to make money.

Banks have two basic functions. The first is that they loan money to individuals, organizations, or businesses.

Suppose that Ms. Garcia wants a new car but cannot pay the entire $28,000 purchase price with the money she has on hand. She will likely apply for a loan at a local bank or credit union. (A credit union operates like a bank but is a nonprofit organization run and owned by the people who use it.) If Ms. Garcia is approved for the loan, the bank or credit union will give her the money she needs to buy the car. In exchange, Ms. Garcia must make monthly payments to the financial institution until the loan has been paid off—a period that usually lasts three to five years, depending on the size of the loan and the borrower's financial health.

But Ms. Garcia is not simply responsible for repaying the principal on the loan—that is, the exact amount of money she borrowed. Suppose that she makes a down payment of $6,000 on the car. That leaves $22,000 that Ms. Garcia must repay. For the privilege of using the funds belonging to the bank or credit union, however, Ms. Garcia is required to pay interest on the loan: she must pay the bank a percentage of the money she borrowed in addition to repaying the original amount of the loan. If she pays 6 percent interest a year and takes five years to pay off the loan, she will eventually pay more than $25,500 on the original $22,000 principal, with interest payments amounting to slightly more than $3,500.

The second function of a bank is related to the first. In order to loan money out, banks must have money coming in. They get this money by encouraging individuals and corporations to deposit funds with them. These funds are placed in special accounts. It is easy for customers to get their money out of these accounts. Customers are able to withdraw cash from their accounts, or they may use debit cards or checks to pay for merchandise, with the money being automatically deducted from their accounts. By the same token, customers can add money to their accounts at any point as well. Customers may be charged penalties if they spend more money than they have in their accounts, but as long as they keep close track of how much money they have, that should not be a major concern.

Bank Accounts and Saving

Banks and credit unions not only charge interest on the money they lend to borrowers, but they offer interest payments on the funds their customers deposit as well. The amount of money paid in interest, however, is

The Financial Samurai

Although some financial experts recommend that people buy certificates of deposit with some or all of their savings, others disagree. One of these naysayers is an anonymous blogger called the Financial Samurai, or Sam. In a post published on his blog in 2013, Sam explained that he had once been an enthusiastic buyer of CDs. Ever since finishing college, he reported, he had put about 30 percent of his savings into CDs. At the time, interest rates on CDs hovered around 4 percent a year; thus, Sam was making $4 for every $100 he put into CDs.

More recently, however, Sam has changed his stance. The low interest rates of the mid-2010s, as he sees it, make CDs much less appealing than they once were. Low interest rates also lead to another problem: if interest rates rise, people with existing CDs will be unable to benefit, as their money will be stuck in a lower-interest certificate. It is better, in Sam's estimation, to have a lower interest rate and the ability to remove money from the account at any time.

quite small. In early 2015 the typical savings account at a bank or credit union offered interest rates of just 0.15 percent per year. If a consumer used $100 to open an account at that interest rate and left the money there for a year, the account would earn about 15¢ in interest. An initial deposit of $1,000, similarly, would bring in just $1.50 of interest. To earn $15 in interest within a year, the consumer would have to deposit about $10,000. And though an interest rate of 0.15 percent sounds—and is—quite low, by early 2016 the average interest rate offered to depositors had dropped even further.

Interest rates on savings accounts at banks and credit unions can vary. By shopping around, savers may be able to find interest rates several times higher than the national average. A website called GOBankingRates, for example, lists some of the best interest rates offered by banks and credit unions at any given time. Experts recommend that account holders check this site or a similar one to ensure that they are getting reasonable rates of interest. "Without comparing rates, you may be shortchanging yourself," says banker Sue Davis-Gillis in an article on the Bankrate website. The best available rates on savings accounts as of early 2016 were only about 1 percent a year, which would earn savers just $1 on every $100 deposited. But though these rates are scarcely favorable to savers, they are considerably higher than the standard rates offered by most financial institutions today.

Low interest levels are frustrating for many bank customers, who would, of course, prefer to have their money earn more for them. Still, credit unions and banks have no

"Without comparing rates, you may be shortchanging yourself."

—Banker Sue Davis-Gillis on interest rates paid on savings accounts shortage of customers. One reason is because twenty-first-century America is a place where money has largely become virtual. Younger people, in particular, have little use for cash. More and more Americans of all ages use debit cards for purchases and pay bills via the Internet. Since both activities generally require the services of a bank or other financial institution, opening an account at a bank or credit union is critical. Equally important, though, is the fact that putting money in an account at a financial institution keeps it safe. Nearly all deposit accounts are insured by the federal government, but cash cannot be replaced if it is lost, stolen, or destroyed.

Many workers also use banks to implement a pay-yourself-first strategy. Most large employers, and some smaller ones, can send paychecks directly to the banks where employees keep their money. Workers sometimes ask that the money from their paychecks be sent to two different accounts. One of these accounts is used strictly for day-to-day expenses, and the other is for savings. A teacher who wants to save $200 from a twice-monthly paycheck of $1,950, say, might ask school officials to send $1,750 to his day-to-day account, with the remaining $200 going into the smaller account. Since that $200 is out of sight, the teacher will not be as tempted to spend it as he might be if it were more easily available. Indeed, customers can set up savings accounts so that they are not connected to a debit card, forcing them to make a special trip to the bank or credit union in order to access the money.

Certificates of Deposit

Because the amount of interest earned in the typical bank savings account is so low, people often look for

Compound Interest

On the surface, interest paid by a bank on a savings account should be very easy to calculate. Suppose that Damon deposits $500 in an account that earns 1 percent interest annually. One percent of $500 is $5, so Damon's account should grow by $5 every year. After one year he would have $505, after two years $510, and so on.

However, that is not how bank accounts work. The reason is compound interest. When interest is compounded, the interest already paid is included when calculating the next interest payment. In the example above, suppose that Damon's bank compounds interest once a year. After one year Damon will, as before, get $5 in interest added to his account for a total of $505. With compound interest, though, $505 becomes the base used to compute the interest payment in the second year. Thus, Damon will receive 1 percent of $505, or $5.05. The difference seems negligible, and in this case it is. However, when interest rates are higher, the effects of compound interest are easier to see. And even when the interest rates are small, the effect becomes quite noticeable after a longer period of time.

ways of making their money grow more quickly. One way for savers to increase their interest rates is to buy a certificate of deposit (CD). Most often offered through banks and credit unions, CDs are similar to regular savings accounts in that they almost always pay a guaranteed rate of interest. Thus, the money used to buy a CD *will* increase. At the same time, CDs are different from ordinary accounts. Customers with regular savings accounts can withdraw their money at any time, but people who purchase CDs must leave the money in the account for a specified period of time. This period of time, which is usually at least three months and can be much longer, is called a *term*.

Because the bank knows exactly how long it will have use of a CD buyer's money, it is willing to offer slightly higher rates of interest on CDs than on regular savings accounts. In general, the longer the term of a CD, the higher the interest paid. Whereas a CD with a three-month term might offer an interest rate of just 0.4 percent, a CD with a term of three years might carry a rate two or three times as high. The rate of a CD can also be dependent on the amount of money a saver puts into the plan. Customers who put more than $10,000 into a CD, for example, may qualify for a higher rate of interest than customers who put in less.

> "Certificates of deposit . . . make financial sense for people of all ages who want a low-risk investment to park cash they don't plan to use immediately."
>
> —*The* Wall Street Journal

Despite the relatively low rates of interest offered by most CDs, financial advisers nonetheless do recommend them to customers who are looking to save. As an article in the *Wall Street Journal* puts it, "Certificates of deposit . . . make financial sense for people of all ages who want a low-risk investment to park cash they don't plan to use immediately." Suppose that a couple is planning a cruise that will cost $5,000, and the first payments will need to be made in September. If their savings account contains the full $5,000 the previous January, they may find it helpful to use that money to buy a nine-month CD at that point instead of leaving the funds in their savings account. The interest rate on the CD will be somewhat higher, which will give them a little more in interest than the savings account would offer. Moreover, since the money in the CD is not easily accessible, they will be less likely to spend it in other ways. Another good use for a CD would be in the case of a person who hopes to save enough money to buy a new car two or three years in the future.

There is one caution to the use of CDs, however. People who purchase CDs must be very sure that they will not need the money in question during the term of the certificate. It is possible to withdraw the money from a CD early, but doing so incurs a penalty. That penalty can vary. If a customer opens a CD with a term of one year or more, the bank will often impose a penalty of three to six months' worth of interest for early withdrawal. Closing the CD after six months, then, can result in the loss of all interest payments. And if the customer has held on to the CD for less than three months, the bank is allowed to keep some of the money originally used to buy the CD. Customers who buy a long-term CD, only to close it after two months, can expect to get back less money than they paid.

The trend in the banking industry, however, is toward larger penalties for early withdrawal. In recent years both Chase and Bank of America, for example, have sharply increased the penalties they charge customers who try to close their CDs before their terms end. Gregg McNelly, a Bank of America customer who had purchased a $10,000 CD, discovered that he needed some of that money for medical expenses. He anticipated that he would need to forfeit some of the interest he had earned. He was shocked to discover that the bank would charge him a fee of $25 plus 3 percent of the money withdrawn—in his case, $325, far more than the standard three to six months of interest. "My jaw dropped when I heard how much it would cost," says

McNelly in an interview with the *Los Angeles Times.* "I can't believe they wanted to charge me so much of my own money just to get my own money." In the end, discouraged by the high penalty, McNelly found the money he needed elsewhere and left the CD untouched.

Certificates of deposit, savings accounts, and the like do not pay much in interest. Nonetheless, they are popular among people who wish to save money. The convenience of opening a bank account is one reason for this popularity. A second reason is the knowledge that interest payments, however small, will increase the amount of money being deposited. And putting money into an account or a CD can keep the money being deposited out of the saver's general fund. It is much easier not to spend money if it is not in the same account used for paying bills. For all these reasons, consumers continue to seek out the savings plans offered by financial institutions.

Chapter Four

The Stock Market

Savings accounts and certificates of deposit have one characteristic that very much appeals to savers: a guaranteed rate of return. If money is deposited into one of these accounts and left there for a reasonable period of time, it will grow—although not by much. The security of knowing that the principal cannot shrink provides peace of mind to people who absolutely cannot risk losing any of their money.

For many people, however, the lack of risk in a CD or savings account does not make up for the fact that the money in the account increases so slowly. Plenty of Americans want—and need—a higher rate of return than the typical bank account can offer. To get a higher return, they must be willing to take on some amount of risk. This is a trade-off: they risk losing some or even all of their funds in exchange for possibly increasing their principal by much larger amounts. People who are looking for higher potential rewards often choose to invest their money—and one of the oldest and most common ways of investing is by buying stocks.

Stocks

The United States is home to millions of businesses. Some of these are very small; they are owned and staffed by just one person with occasional help from a part-time worker. People who offer handyman services, for example, often fall into this category; they do simple home repairs and hire assistants when the jobs require a second pair of hands. Slightly larger companies, such as legal offices, independent pharmacies, and vehicle repair shops, may have anywhere from a handful of full-time employees up to a few dozen. Like their smaller counterparts, they are typically owned outright by a single person or by a group of two or three partners. Businesses of this size are often referred to as small businesses.

When most Americans think of business, however, they think of much larger corporations, such as car manufacturers Ford and General Motors, technology companies like Apple and Microsoft, and well-known retailers like Walmart, McDonald's, and Home Depot. These companies employ thousands of workers, earn enormous profits each year, and often have a presence throughout the United States and beyond. As of early 2016, for example, technology manufacturer IBM had more than 375,000 employees, grocery chain Whole Foods reported close to $13 billion in profits, and Staples, which specializes in selling office supplies, operated more than 1,500 stores in the United States and Canada. Compared to a small catering business or a local roofing company, these corporations are enormous.

Most of the largest American companies are publicly traded—that is, they are owned not by individuals or small partnerships but rather by many different people. In essence, ownership of these companies is divided

into billions of pieces—and sometimes trillions. These pieces are known as shares of stock, and they can be bought and sold by anyone who wishes to invest money. An investor who owns one hundred shares of stock in Microsoft, for example, is technically part owner of the company. Since there are more than 5 trillion shares of Microsoft stock currently in existence, people with only one hundred shares own such a tiny percentage of the company that they have no real say in how the business is run. However, the purpose of buying stock in a publicly traded company is not to make decisions for the corporation. Rather, it is to make money—and at a rate much faster than any savings account or certificate of deposit can match.

How the Market Works

Publicly traded companies are listed in a stock exchange, a virtual or physical marketplace where shares of stock can be bought and sold. Each company has its own set of initials for easy identification: Starbucks, for example, is listed as SBUX; communications and entertainment company Time Warner is referred to as TWX: and GEIMX indicates energy and industrial giant General Electric. Shares of stock are constantly being traded—that is, sold or purchased—through these exchanges. No individual person or organization sets the price. Instead, the cost of a share of stock in any given company is set by the market. In other words, the cost is determined by the amount a buyer is willing to pay for a share and how much a seller is willing to take for it.

Say that Ms. O'Neill wishes to buy two hundred shares of stock in a particular company. She or her broker—a person who buys and sells stocks on behalf of others—checks the price of the stock and discovers that the cost per share is $3.50. To buy two hundred shares of this company's stock, then, would cost Ms. O'Neill roughly 200 multiplied by $3.50, or $700. If she is using a broker, and most investors do, she would also have to pay a fee to the broker for carrying out the transaction. This might be a specified amount for a single purchase of any size, or it might be calculated as a percentage of what Ms. O'Neill spends. Thus, Ms. O'Neill would probably pay closer to $710 or $720 rather than the $700 selling price of the stock.

Ms. O'Neill has two possible ways of making money from her investment. The first has to do with what the company chooses to do with the money it makes each year, or its profits. Assuming companies make a profit at

From Lemonade to Stock Investments

A Canadian high school student named Julian Marchese became interested in stocks when he was eight. Like many children that age, he had set up a lemonade stand that had brought him some money. Unlike others, Marchese wondered what he might be able to do with the money besides spending it. A little research on the Internet led him to information about the stock market. He found the information intriguing and set out to learn more; soon he was determined to invest as much of his lemonade profits as he could.

Though just seventeen, Marchese has become a thoughtful and experienced investor. He is especially interested in what is known as global macro strategy, in which investors try to predict the ups and downs of foreign markets based on each country's political and economic situation. Marchese sees his interest in stocks not as a hobby but rather as a potential livelihood. He plans to study finance in college and then find a job managing a hedge fund—a partnership of investors who are interested in high-risk investment strategies. For Marchese, then, lemonade was not merely a thirst quencher on a hot summer day; it was a path to a career.

all, company officials may choose to give some percentage of the profits directly to the shareholders. These payments are called dividends, and they are parceled out to investors according to the number of shares of stock they own. The amount of a dividend can vary considerably. In this example, Ms. O'Neill might receive a total yearly dividend of around $15—but it could be much less or somewhat more depending on the size of the company, the amount of profit, and the willingness of company leaders to distribute profits to shareholders at all rather than using the extra money to expand the company.

Reward

For the typical investor, dividends are relatively small; and as mentioned, many companies rarely if ever distribute profits in this way. Most investors argue instead that the real value of buying stocks is the expectation that the value of the shares will rise over the next few weeks, months, or years. If the company in which Ms. O'Neill holds stock does well financially, such as by expanding its operations or by making accurate predictions about how best to make money, it will attract the attention of new investors, and the price of its shares will probably increase. In two years, perhaps, the cost of a single share of the stock may rise from $3.50 to $5. Ms. O'Neill can now sell her two hundred shares of stock for 200 multiplied by $5, or $1,000. Even after subtracting the fees she must pay her broker both as a buyer and as a seller, she has done well: her initial investment of $700 has turned into $1,000 in just two years. There is no way $700 could have earned her anywhere near $300 in that time if she had placed it in a bank account.

"Investors willing to stick with stocks over long periods of time . . . generally have been rewarded with strong, positive returns."

—Financial website Investor.gov.

Buying and selling stocks may seem, then, like an excellent strategy for making money, and in many ways it is. Over time, stock prices do tend to rise—and faster than the typical interest rate paid by CDs and savings accounts. As an article on the website Investor.gov puts it, "Investors willing to stick with stocks over long periods of time, say 15 years, generally have been rewarded with strong, positive returns." Statistically speaking, an investor who put $10,000 into the stock market in 2001, say, now has more money than he or she would have if that money had been put into a bank account instead.

Moreover, some investors have used the stock market to become extremely rich. Many people have fantasies of discovering a small, unknown company and buying much of its stock for very little money—only to have the stock price soar when the company turns into a modern-day version of Microsoft, Apple, or IBM. Although stories like these are unusual, some people do make a good deal of money by investing in this way. As a teenager, for example, Brandon Fleisher of Ontario, Canada, helped his parents buy stocks worth $48,000 for investment purposes. Fleisher kept careful track of each stock, selling when he thought the price of shares was due to drop and buying new stocks instead that he thought were about to jump in value. Two years later, through judicious buying and selling, Fleisher turned that initial $48,000 into $147,000—more than triple what he started with. "Investing is something I love to do," Fleisher told an interviewer for a profile on the CNNMoney website.

> "Investing is something I love to do."
>
> —Teenage stock investor Brandon Fleisher

Risk

But the stock market has a downside as well. There is never any guarantee that stock prices will rise. In fact, if a sluggish economy or poor decisions force a retailer to close stores or a manufacturer to cut back on production, the value of that company's stock will likely drop. "Any stock can lose value," points out an article on CNN's website. An investor who bought three hundred shares of a company's stock at $25.50 per share may discover that each share is worth just $17 a few weeks or months later. The investor is now faced with a decision: keep the stock in hopes that its value will return to at least the original $25.50, if not more, or sell before the stock can drop further—and lose hundreds of dollars on the deal.

Investment Clubs

For many years, people interested in the stock market have formed investment clubs. In some of these organizations, members pool their money and decide together what companies to invest in. In others, members make their own investing decisions but swap information and opinions about companies whose stocks seem promising. In each instance, the focus is on combining the wisdom and knowledge of each member for the good of the group.

Investment clubs are much more common among adults than among high school students. In part, that is because people cannot legally trade stocks until they are eighteen years old. Some schools, however, do have clubs in which participants use play money to make and track hypothetical investments or where an adult is willing to invest real money on the students' behalf. At the Greenhill School in Dallas, Texas, alumni raised $100,000 so students in an investment club could buy actual stocks. The students chose to diversify by buying shares of corporations as varied as power supplier Duke Energy, communications giant AT&T, and medical manufacturer Johnson & Johnson. The goal was to make money—and to understand the workings of the stock market in a real-world situation.

Indeed, economic conditions can often raise or lower the prices of virtually all stocks at once. The Great Depression of the 1930s, an economic calamity in which poverty was widespread and a quarter or more of Americans were thrown out of work, was sparked in part by the collapse of the stock market in late 1929. Many stocks lost nearly all their value during that period; some could not be sold at any price. Similarly, toward the end of 2008 stock prices underwent a sharp drop, causing many investors to lose whatever gains they had made in the previous few years. On a single September day in 2008, stocks lost an average of 9 percent of their value. A typical share that had sold for $100 that morning went for just $91 at the close of the day. "People started to sell and they sold hard," one trader explained in an interview with the *New York Times*. "It didn't matter what you had—you sold."

> **"When you invest in the stock market, you're betting on the ability of businesses to continue being innovative and efficient over the years."**
>
> —*British newspaper the Guardian*

Nor are steep drops in stock prices a thing of the past. More recently, January 2016 was a bad month for the market. According to one estimate, 93 percent of investors in the stock market saw the value of their shares drop that month. Experts caution investors that ups and downs are a natural phenomenon in the stock market, and it is unwise to react too strongly to sudden changes. Still, investors have trouble heeding this advice. Some sell their stocks as soon as the value begins to drop, fearing that the company may go bankrupt—which would make the stock worthless. Others refuse to sell their shares until the price has rebounded to the level it was when the investor bought them to begin with—a moment that might never arrive.

Even with the ups and downs, the stock market can be a wise investment for people who can afford to take the long view. Investors who remember that setbacks are natural and do not react with dread when their holdings lose ground can—and probably will—continue to make money in the stock market. "Don't panic," advises an article in the British newspaper the *Guardian,* focusing on how investors should respond to sudden and unexpected drops in stock value. "When you invest in the stock market, you're betting on the ability of businesses to continue being innovative and efficient over the years." As long as companies do their jobs well, investors in the stock market can expect to reap the benefits.

Chapter Five

Bonds and Mutual Funds

The stock market is attractive to many investors because of the potential for earning high yields. Doubling, tripling, or even quadrupling a stock investment in a year or less can happen—and often does. Not all investors are quite so enthusiastic, however. In particular, some investors steer away from the stock market because they are unwilling to risk big losses—and investing in a single stock, or even a few stocks, leaves open the possibility that an entire investment could be lost. In her book *Mistake Power*, author Juliana Vilke describes buying many shares of stock in a company called eToys—which went out of business not long after her purchase. "I lost my entire investment," Vilke writes. For plenty of investors, Vilke's story is a cautionary tale—a warning against investing too heavily in the stock market.

Bonds

Many investors, then, are looking for a middle ground. They want more than the limited interest payments

A construction worker inspects repair work being done on a bridge in Oregon. When people buy government-issued bonds they earn interest from their purchases while also helping to raise money for large-scale projects such as road and bridge repairs.

offered by a CD or savings account but prefer to avoid the risks of the stock market. For some of these investors, bonds represent an excellent compromise. Bonds are certificates issued most often by corporations or by state, local, or federal governments and sold to investors. The purpose, from the issuer's perspective, is to raise money quickly and easily—and in the case of governments, to avoid needing to increase taxes. From the investor's point of view, the goal is to earn more than a standard bank account can offer but with less risk than investing in stocks. Both issuer and investor, then, can benefit from the bond market. "At their best, bonds are a win-win deal," writes financial columnist Matthew Lubanko in the *Hartford Courant* newspaper.

Like certificates of deposit and ordinary bank accounts, bonds are essentially a loan. People buying bonds are providing a quick infusion of cash to the government or business issuing the certificates. That money will be used to fund various projects. In the case of corporations, the money from sales of bonds might enable the company to buy another business, begin a major expansion into new territory, or break ground for a state-of-the-art manufacturing plant. Governments, similarly, may use funds from bond sales for the purpose of building sports arenas, repairing roads and bridges, or cleaning up an environmentally damaged area. In exchange for the use of their money, purchasers receive interest payments from the bond issuer. Generally speaking, the level of interest from buying a bond is higher than an investor could expect to get from any savings account at a bank or credit union.

> "At their best, bonds are a win-win deal."
>
> —Financial columnist Matthew Lubanko

Differences in Bonds

Bonds are not all alike, however. They come in a wide variety of forms. Municipal bonds are issued by towns, cities, and occasionally other governments, and corporate bonds are issued by private industries. Some bonds are taxable—that is, the amount an investor pays for the bond is subject to taxation. Yet other bonds, notably those issued by governments and nonprofit organizations like hospitals, are tax-exempt. That means buyers need not pay taxes on their purchase, at least not right away.

Another way in which bonds differ has to do with risk. Most bonds issued by governments are guaranteed. As with most certificates of deposit, buyers of government bonds typically cannot lose money on their purchases. Corporate bonds, on the other hand, do carry risk. It is always a possibility that the company issuing a specific bond will go bankrupt and be unable to meet its obligations. This is known as defaulting on the bond, and it costs buyers their entire investment. The chance of default, though, is relatively small, especially if investors buy bonds issued by reputable companies. On average, only about 4 percent of corporate bonds from these types of firms ever default.

Finally, some bonds must be kept for many years before they pay their full value to the investor, but others can be cashed in after a matter of months. Given this degree of variation, bonds are grouped into categories that can be hard even for experts to distinguish: original-issue discount bonds, insured bonds, zero-coupon bonds, pre-refunded bonds, and many, many more. Any of these bonds can be a part of an investor's plans for making money.

Savings Bonds

The most widespread and familiar type of bond in America is the Series EE US Savings Bond. Issued by the federal government, Series EE bonds have a reputation for steady, if small, increases in value over the years. They

The World's First Mutual Fund

In 1774 a Dutch businessman named Adriaan Van Ketwich set up an investment organization much like a modern mutual fund. At the time, Europe was beginning to emerge from a financial downturn that had badly affected investment. The downturn had reduced wealth across the continent and driven less-wealthy investors out of the market. Van Ketwich's fund, which he called Eendragt Maakt Magt (Unity Creates Strength), pooled the money of hundreds of investors and diversified by investing the pooled funds in a wide variety of business opportunities, including some in places as distant as Central and South America.

Van Ketwich's brainchild was reasonably successful at first but became less profitable when war broke out between England and the Netherlands a few years later. Thereafter the fund made few if any investments. Still, it was not formally closed until 1824. Most economic historians consider Unity Creates Strength to be the world's first mutual fund.

are often used toward the purchase of big-ticket items such as cars, homes, and college educations. Kathy, a woman from upstate New York, was able to pay for college partly by cashing in Series EE bonds her grandparents had purchased for her when she was small. Savings bonds are also used often for presents and rewards. Several credit card companies offer their cardholders savings bonds if they regularly charge purchases to their credit cards, for example. Series EE bonds are described by financial planner Marc S. Freedman in a *Time* magazine article as "gifts that grandparents and other relatives give children to commemorate life events such as a birthday, first communion, or a Bar Mitzvah."

The point of buying a savings bond is the knowledge that the value of the bond will eventually double. The speed at which the doubling takes place, however, varies according to the prevailing interest rate at the time the bond is purchased. As of spring 2016, a bond purchased for $100 will be worth $200 in 2036, twenty years after purchase. A bond purchased in an earlier year, when interest rates were higher, might take less time to double its value, but the standard for current investors is about twenty years.

That does not mean, however, that the bond must remain untouched for twenty years—or that it must be cashed in immediately when the value has doubled. A savings bond gains in value, even if only slightly, every year. Beginning one year after purchase, a person who holds a bond can exchange it for its present value at any point, though doing so before the twenty-year mark will sacrifice a few months' worth of interest. At the other end of the scale, the bond actually collects interest for thirty years, so it will eventually be worth more than double what was paid for it. Holding on to the bond for an extra five or ten years may turn out to be in the best interest of the bondholder.

Like CDs but unlike the stock exchange, savings bonds are fully guaranteed. A savings bond purchased for $1,000 in January 2018 *will* have a value of at least $2,000 when January 2038 comes along. And the interest rate for a bond tends to be better than for a savings account or a CD. But though the interest rate is higher, it is not sufficiently higher to attract investors who long for a bigger payoff. Today, a savings bond held for twenty years earns about 3.5 percent interest each year, a figure that is not nearly what a canny investor in the stock market might manage to get. But though bonds in general are not as lucrative as many investors would like, US savings bonds remain quite popular among some investors, especially older ones who remember when interest rates were high and bonds took less time to double in value.

Mutual Funds

Mutual funds are a type of investment program in which the money of hundreds or thousands of investors is pooled. Various investors buy into the fund, which is managed by professionals in the field of finance. These experts invest the combined money of all the fund's members. Some of the money may go into stocks, with the stocks nearly always being issued by a variety of corporations across a number of different industries. The money may also be used to buy bonds of different types, term lengths, and degree of risk. And some of the money may be invested in other ways as well, such as by purchasing real estate.

The idea behind mutual funds is that investors should diversify their holdings—that is, they lower their risk when they buy a mix of stocks, bonds, and other investments. As a popular adage quoted on Investor. gov expresses it, "Don't put all your eggs in one basket." Countless investors over the years have discovered that people who buy stock in just one corporation may suffer financially if economic conditions change. The energy

> "Don't put all your eggs in one basket."
>
> —An old adage on Investor.gov encouraging diversification in investment

company Enron, for example, went out of business in 2001 after a series of bad decisions and some illegal activities on the part of its leaders. As the company moved toward bankruptcy, stock shares that had once traded for $90 apiece suddenly were worth less than a dollar—and before long they were worth nothing at all. Mutual funds spread out the risk by investing members' money in many different stocks and by placing some of their holdings in bonds and other investments as well.

Socially Conscious Funds

The diversification of mutual funds is attractive to many investors. For some, however, it presents a problem. For moral and political reasons, investors do not always approve of certain companies. Many investors would not buy shares of stock in a tobacco company, for example, as they do not wish to support the manufacture of cigarettes. That can make it difficult to own shares in a mutual fund. Investors rarely know which stocks the experts who manage the funds have picked, and there is usually no guarantee that certain types of companies are excluded. The primary goal of a mutual fund, after all, is to make money rather than to set political policy.

People who are strongly against investing in certain companies, however, can buy into mutual funds known for their support of social responsibility. Faced with a decision of investing in a tobacco company or a business specializing in medical supplies, for instance, a traditional mutual fund manager will choose whichever stock seems likely to bring in the most money. A manager of a socially responsible fund, however, would pick the medical supply company. Today, hundreds of mutual funds promise to avoid investing in certain types of corporations.

This ability to reduce the risk of investing—while still benefiting from potential increases in the value of stocks—attracts many investors to mutual funds. The other draw of mutual funds is professional management. It can be difficult for ordinary people to determine how best to distribute their money among stocks, bonds, and other possible investments. Few Americans have the time, inclination, or experience necessary to determine whether it is better to invest in a young company with great growth potential or in a more settled business with a strong reputation. Few know enough to decide which of several corporate bonds currently on the market is likely to have the highest value five or ten years in the future. Instead of doing the research on these companies themselves, many people prefer to have experts make those decisions for them. The difference, says financial adviser Jonathan Murray in an interview with the *Baltimore Sun,* is "like flying a plane yourself, or hiring an experienced pilot."

Mutual funds are often recommended by financial advisers. As an article on Zacks puts it, "Mutual funds are great options for investors looking for a relatively less risky way to earn at least more than what fixed income instruments [such as bonds] offer." Mutual funds are popular among customers, too. As of 2016, about 90 million Americans had at least some money invested in a mutual fund, and the total holdings of all the mutual funds in the United States amounted to more than $13 trillion in all. By most accounts, moreover, these figures are growing.

How Mutual Funds Work

Much like stocks, mutual funds are divided into shares. People who wish to buy into a mutual fund are actually buying a part of the fund, just as people who want to buy stock in a company are purchasing a small slice of ownership. An investment of $500 in a particular fund, for instance, might buy an investor ten or twelve shares of the fund. When the fund does well, the value of the share grows. If the fund loses money, the value of each share shrinks. Buying and selling fund shares is simple and quick. Investors usually can buy into a mutual fund for a few hundred dollars, and investors can redeem their shares at any time just by selling them back to the fund at current market prices.

Unlike stocks, however, mutual funds charge fees to their investors. These fees cover the expenses of making stock market trades and the salaries of the professionals who manage the fund and decide which investments to buy and sell. The exact fees charged by a given fund can vary, but a reasonable rule of thumb is that fees amount to about 1 percent of each investor's holdings a year. Thus, an investor with shares worth $30,000 might expect to pay $300 in fees. However, fees for different funds can differ greatly, and a higher fee does not necessarily imply a more successful fund. When deciding which of several mutual funds to buy, investors are advised to take the fees each fund charges into consideration. It is also pos-sible to avoid some fees by keeping a minimum amount of money in a fund. Vanguard, a financial services com-pany that sells mutual funds, waives certain fees for cus-tomers with balances above $10,000.

Mutual funds are not intended to be guaranteed sources of income, and they are not. Like a share of stock, the value of a mutual fund can—and does—go up and down along with the rest of the stock market. The drops in stock value may or may not be offset by steady gains among the bonds purchased by the mutual funds.

In short-term situations—that is, over a period of weeks or months—it is easy to lose money in even the best-managed mutual funds. When Enron went bankrupt, for example, a lot of mutual fund owners suffered because their funds had purchased more Enron stock than was wise. Still, the average mutual fund tries to cushion investors from the biggest swings of the market by diversifying its purchases. Between stocks, bonds, and mutual funds, most people can find investments that they like.

Glossary

bonds: Interest-paying investment certificates issued by governments or corporations.

certificate of deposit (CD): A savings tool in which buyers receive interest.

diversifying: Buying a number of different investments and different types of investments.

dividend: A share of profits paid by corporations to their owners.

financial institution: A bank, credit union, or other business that offers loans and deposits.

fixed expenses: Costs, such as for housing, that do not vary much from month to month.

interest: Money paid by a bank or borrower for the privilege of using someone else's money.

mutual fund: An investment program in which funds belonging to many different people are pooled.

recession: An economic slowdown or downturn.

sales tax: Money paid to a government when people make purchases.

share of stock: Ownership of a piece of a corporation.

variable expenses: Costs, such as for entertainment, that fluctuate each month.

For More Information

Books

David W. Bianchi, *Blue Chip Kids: What Every Child (and Parent) Should Know About Money, Investing, and the Stock Market.* New York: Wiley, 2015.

Tammy Gagne, *A Teen Guide to Saving and Investing.* Hockessin, DE: Mitchell Lane, 2016.

Kara McGuire, *Making Money Work.* Mankato, MN: Compass Point, 2014.

Rick Roman, *I'm a Shareholder Kit: The Basics About Stocks.* Gilbert, AZ: Leading Edge Gifts, 2012.

Internet Sources

Tony Armstrong, "What Is a CD (Certificate of Deposit)?," *Banking* (blog), NerdWallet, February 29, 2016. www .nerdwallet.com/blog/banking/cd-certificate-of-deposit.

Bank of America, "Money Management for Teens." www.bankofamerica.com/deposits/manage/money -management-for-teens.go.

Commonwealth Bank of Australia, "Savings Tips for Teens." www.commbank.com.au/personal/can/bank ing-for-teenagers/saving-tips.html.

Patrick Gillespie, "Meet the 17-Year-Old Investor Who Tripled His Money," CNNMoney, April 28, 2015. http://

money.cnn.com/2015/04/28/investing/millennial-inves
tor-17-year-old-brandon-fleisher/.

Julia LaRoche, "The 20 Under 20: Meet the Teen Trad-
ers Trying to Take Over the Finance World," Business Insider, November 8, 2013. www.businessinsider.com/20
-under-20-in-finance-2013-11.

Kimberly Palmer, "10 Money Tips for Teens," U.S. News
Money, November 5, 2014. http://money.usnews.com/
money/personal-finance/articles/2014/11/05/10-mon
ey-tips-for-teens.

Andrew Sather, "5 Tips of Investment Advice for Teenagers," Investing for Beginners 101 (blog), December 11,
2014. http://einvestingforbeginners.com/2014/12/11/5
-tips-investment-advice-teenagers.

Security Industry and Financial Markets Association,
"Bond Basics." www.investinginbonds.com/learnmore
.asp?catid=46.

Spencer Tierney and Melissa Lambarena, "What Is a
Savings Account?," Banking (blog), NerdWallet, March
29, 2016. www.nerdwallet.com/blog/banking/savings
-accounts-basics.

US Securities and Exchange Commission, "Invest Wise-
ly: An Introduction to Mutual Funds." www.sec.gov/inve
stor/pubs/inwsmf.htm.

Websites

Investor.gov (www.investor.gov). A project of the US
Securities and Exchange Commission, this site provides
information about choosing and monitoring investments.
It explains how to invest, why to invest, and how the
process of investment works.

Security Industry and Financial Markets Association (www.investinginbonds.com). This site offers information about bonds and how they work, including a discussion of how bonds might best fit into a larger investment strategy.

TheMint (www.themint.org). This website provides plenty of information, activities, and games about economics and money. It also offers finance tips for teens, including information about saving, spending, and investing. It is run by financial planning company Northwestern Mutual.

T. Rowe Price (http://individual.troweprice.com). This financial website provides information regarding stocks and bonds, how to invest, the difference between saving and investing, and more.

Games

Road Trip to Savings (http://practicalmoneyskills.com/games/road_trip/road_trip.html). A game that involves moving cash into savings while still paying necessary expenses.

Stock Market Game (www.howthemarketworks.com). A game that models the way the stock market works.

Virtual Stock Exchange (www.marketwatch.com/game). An online game that allows players to collaborate in buying and tracking virtual stocks.

Index

Picture Credits

About the Author

Stephen Currie has written dozens of books for children and young adults. His works for ReferencePoint Press include *Goblins*, *Women World Leaders*, and *The Renaissance*. He has also taught at grade levels ranging from kindergarten to college. He lives in New York's Hudson Valley.